100 Essential Forms for New Teachers

A Must-Have Collection of Checklists, Planning Sheets, Assessments, and More That Puts All the Forms You Need at Your Fingertips

Linda Ward Beech

New York ○ Toronto ○ London ○ Auckland ○ Sydney
New Delhi ○ Mexico City ○ Hong Kong ○ Buenos Aires

The following pages adapted from:

The New Teacher's Complete Sourcebook: Middle School, Scholastic Teaching Resources: 10, 13, 14, 26, 30, 83, 89, 108, 109

The New Teacher's Complete Sourcebook: Grades K–4, Scholastic Teaching Resources: 12, 22, 24, 86

Learning to Teach...Not Just for Beginners, Scholastic Teaching Resources: 16, 18, 19, 32, 88, 90, 97, 112, 115

Super Start-the-Year Book, Scholastic Teaching Resources: 27, 28

INSTRUCTOR, January/February 1998: 29

Your Classroom Library: New Ways to Give It More Teaching Power, Scholastic Teaching Resources: 42

Momentum Library: Leveled Independent Reading Practice, Scholastic Teaching Resources: 43, 46, 47, 54, 55, 56, 57, 58, 62, 106

Every Child Can Read, Scholastic Teaching Resources: 50, 51, 53, 87

Learner Support Program, Scholastic Canada, Ltd.: 52

The Study Skills Handbook, Scholastic Teaching Resources: 107

Editor: Mela Ottaiano
Cover design by Jaime Lucero
Interior design by Grafica Inc.
Interior illustrations by Teresa Anderko (pages 8, 31, 40, 66, 95),
Steve Cox (pages 20, 66, 119), Maxie Chambliss (pages 38, 80, 100, 114),
Paige Billin-Frye (page 49)

ISBN: 978-0-545-27349-7

Table of Contents

*Student Reproducible

Table of Contents

*Student Reproducible

Table of Contents

*Student Reproducible

Introduction

When asked what they like best about their occupation, most teachers will say that it's the teaching itself. However, teaching is only part of what teachers do. Classroom instructors spend many hours on an amazing number of other tasks, from decorating their room to keeping track of missing library books.

The purpose of this book is to make these tasks easier by providing 110 essential forms for classroom use. Each of them is available in printed form in this book, and customizable versions are also provided on the CD. (See How to Use the Companion CD, page 7.)

Here is more of what you'll find in the book:

- Checklists that will serve as reminders and help you organize your tasks and time.

- Record-keeping and assessment forms.

- Planning forms—whether you're designing a weekly lesson, setting up your classroom library, or preparing for a substitute.

- Forms that help you get to know students better.

- Forms that students can use for learning.

- Numerous forms that support different areas of the curriculum.

- Forms for field trips.

- Forms to facilitate home-school connections.

Look through the table of contents to see what other forms you might find helpful. By using these reproducibles you can free up more of your time for the best part of your job—teaching!

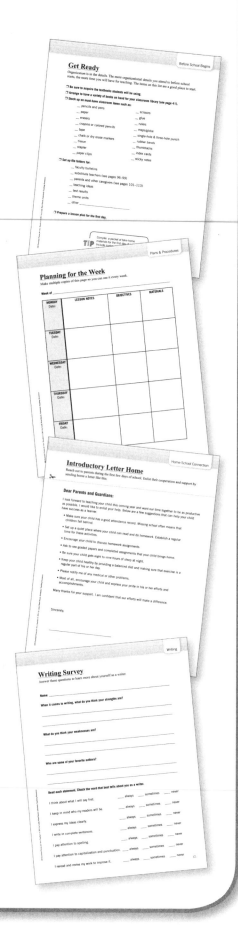

How to Use the Companion CD

The companion CD is a flexible tool that will help simplify your teaching. It contains customizable versions of the majority of forms available as traditional reproducible pages in this book. Photocopy a form or, if you don't have immediate access to a photocopier, simply print multiple copies from the CD.

Make the most of the customizable forms by filling in the various fields before printing. You may also choose to provide prompts or other notes on some of the student learning pages to scaffold assignments as necessary.

The customizable fields will be indicated by highlighting on screen. Note: You must check the "Highlight fields" box to view the highlighted customizable sections. The highlighting will not appear on the printouts.

TIPS

To customize and save the files on the CD, you will need to use Adobe Reader™, version 7.0 or higher. You can find a download that is available free of charge for Mac and PC systems at www.adobe.com/downloads.

As soon as possible, transfer all of the PDF files into a folder on your computer. Taking care of this step in advance will save you time later. It also helps you when you want to save any edited versions for future reference. The CD that comes with the book will always be your master copy.

Use the Tab key to move between the customizable fields, or click directly on a particular field.

Section 1 Before School Begins

Overview: Some of the most important things you do in the classroom will take place before school starts. The forms in this section will help you collect, identify, arrange, organize, anticipate, and prepare key information and tasks.

Page 9: Your Expectations
Use this page as a guide in reflecting and focusing on your role as a teacher.

Pages 10–11: Locate Places; Identify People
Make use of these lists to help familiarize yourself with the school and its key personnel before classes start.

Pages 12–14: School Policies; More About Policies; A Time for Everything
By finding the answers to the questions on these pages, you can assemble a wealth of important information about the policies, regulations, timing, and procedures followed at your school.

Pages 15–16: Get Ready; An Appealing Classroom
For a smooth start, be sure to complete the must-do items on these lists. You might also consult fellow teachers for their ideas.

Page 17: Make a Floor Plan
You can draw your classroom plan on this page. Refer to the checklist to help you remember to sketch the different furniture and other items in your room. Don't be afraid to make changes as your needs change.

Page 18: Safety First
Check with the administration to find out what other safety rules and guidelines apply to your classroom and school.

Page 19: Collect Stuff
Be sure to add your own ideas to this list. Consider sending a list of these and similar materials home to encourage parents to donate to your collection.

Your Expectations

Why are you here? Before you begin the work of preparing for your first day of school, take a moment to think about your role as a teacher.

Why do you want to teach? _____

_____

_____

_____

_____

What are three main things you hope to accomplish this year?

1. _____

_____

2. _____

_____

3. _____

_____

What challenges do you expect to face? _____

_____

_____

_____

In what areas do you expect to need help? How will you seek it? _____

_____

_____

_____

_____

100 Essential Forms for New Teachers © 2011 by Linda Ward Beech, Scholastic Teaching Resources

 TIP Keep a journal of your teaching adventures. You'll be surprised by what you learn during the year.

Locate Places

You'll spend a lot of time at school in the coming months. Make yourself at home by locating these places in and around the building.

❒ **Principal's office**

❒ **Faculty room**

❒ **Faculty mailboxes**

❒ **Faculty restrooms**

❒ **Fire drill exit route**

❒ **School bus pickup area**

❒ **Cafeteria**

❒ **Library**

❒ **Technology center**

❒ **Textbook and supply storage**

❒ **Gymnasium**

❒ **Auditorium**

❒ **Student restrooms**

❒ **Health station**

❒ **Photocopier and fax machine storage**

❒ **Audio-visual equipment storage**

❒ **Parent-teacher room**

TIP

Depending on the transportation you will use to get to school, you may want to locate nearby bus or train stops or the faculty parking area. If using on-street parking, be sure to check for any street regulations.

Identify People

You can't meet everyone at once, but it's a good idea to know the names of important people in your school. Record them here. If available, also include their phone numbers.

Principal: _____

Assistant principal: _____

Office secretary and other staff: _____

_____

Grade-level coordinator: _____

Nurse or health aid: _____

Cafeteria supervisor: _____

Head custodian: _____

School guard or security coordinator: _____

Coach or athletic director: _____

School psychologist or counselor: _____

Speech therapist: _____

Reading specialist: _____

Art specialist: _____

Music specialist: _____

Librarian: _____

Technology specialist: _____

Parent organization leader: _____

Teacher(s) for special needs: _____

Other: _____

School Policies

Each school has its own policies and procedures. Some of these are mandated by the state or local school district; others are put in place by the principal. You'll want to learn as much as you can about the regulations that govern your school. Consult the Internet, school administrators, and fellow teachers to answer these questions.

What are the policies for saluting the flag or other routines to start the school day? _____

_____

_____

How are attendance records handled? _____

_____

Is there a dress code for students? If so, what is it? _____

_____

What are the guidelines for student discipline? _____

_____

What are the procedures for fire drills and other emergencies? _____

_____

What is the policy regarding birthday or holiday parties? _____

_____

What are the procedures for inclement weather? _____

_____

What are the guidelines for sending home parent letters? _____

_____

What guidelines are there for giving homework at your grade level? _____

_____

What are the procedures for obtaining classroom supplies? _____

_____

How do you arrange for a substitute? _____

_____

What are the procedures for scheduling and organizing field trips? _____

_____

100 Essential Forms for New Teachers © 2011 by Linda Ward Beech, Scholastic Teaching Resources

More About Policies

Knowing and following school policies is important for your performance as a teacher. Take the time to find the answers to these questions.

What are your working hours in the school? _____

What procedures should you follow when working after hours or on weekends or holidays in the school? _____
_____
_____

What is the school policy concerning sick days? _____
_____

What is the school policy concerning personal days? _____
_____

What non-classroom teacher duties are expected of you? _____
_____
_____

What is the dress code for teachers? _____
_____
_____

How and when will you be evaluated as a teacher? _____
_____
_____

Will you have a classroom aide or assistant? _____
_____

How can you get mentoring? _____
_____
_____

What roles are teachers expected to take in all-school events such as fairs, assemblies, and student presentations? _____
_____
_____
_____

A Time for Everything

Schools run on a schedule, and your classroom hours will be determined by your school's timetable. Find out when:

your official school day begins and ends _____

the student day begins and ends _____

students are considered tardy _____

school buses arrive and depart _____

attendance must be taken and reported _____

students go to lunch _____

students have recess (if any) _____

students go to special classes such as art, music, physical education, library

_____

_____

specific students get additional support _____

_____

_____

staff meetings are held _____

school closings due to bad weather are announced _____

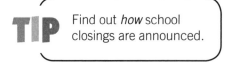

TIP Find out *how* school closings are announced.

100 Essential Forms for New Teachers © 2011 by Linda Ward Beech, Scholastic Teaching Resources

Get Ready

Organization is in the details. The more organizational details you attend to before school starts, the more time you will have for teaching. The items on this list are a good place to start.

❐ **Be sure to acquire the textbooks students will be using.**

❐ **Arrange to have a variety of books on hand for your classroom library (see page 41).**

❐ **Stock up on must-have classroom items such as:**

__ pencils and pens	__ scissors
__ paper	__ glue
__ erasers	__ rulers
__ crayons or colored pencils	__ maps/globe
__ tape	__ single-hole & three-hole punch
__ chalk or dry erase markers	__ rubber bands
__ tissue	__ thumbtacks
__ stapler	__ index cards
__ paper clips	__ sticky notes

❐ **Set up file folders for:**

__ faculty bulletins

__ substitute teachers (see pages 96–99)

__ parents and other caregivers (see pages 101–113)

__ teaching ideas

__ test results

__ theme units

__ other _____

❐ **Prepare a lesson plan for the first day.**

TIP Compile a packet of take-home materials for the first day of school. Include materials such as the Introductory Letter Home on page 101 and the Profile From Home on page 24.

100 Essential Forms for New Teachers © 2011 by Linda Ward Beech, Scholastic Teaching Resources

An Appealing Classroom

You want your classroom to provide a welcoming environment for students. You also want it to be a place organized to support learning. Use this checklist as a guideline for creating both.

❐ **Prepare a catchy bulletin board display.**

❐ **Post a classroom calendar on which you can write upcoming events.**

❐ **Put your name, grade, and room number on the door.**

❐ **Display colorful posters.**

❐ **Set up learning centers.**

❐ **Set up a classroom library.**

❐ **Make student mailboxes.**

❐ **Write your name on the board.**

❐ **Set up computers.**

❐ **Create a storage system for manipulatives and other supplies.**

❐ **Make signs to designate centers, work areas, class library.**

❐ **Be sure to have items such as**

    __ wastebasket and recycling containers

    __ clock

    __ pencil sharpener

TIP Make use of every nook and cranny. You can even hang displays on a clothesline!

100 Essential Forms for New Teachers © 2011 by Linda Ward Beech, Scholastic Teaching Resources

Make a Floor Plan

Arranging a classroom can be challenging. Use the grid on this page to try out possible plans before you start moving furniture.

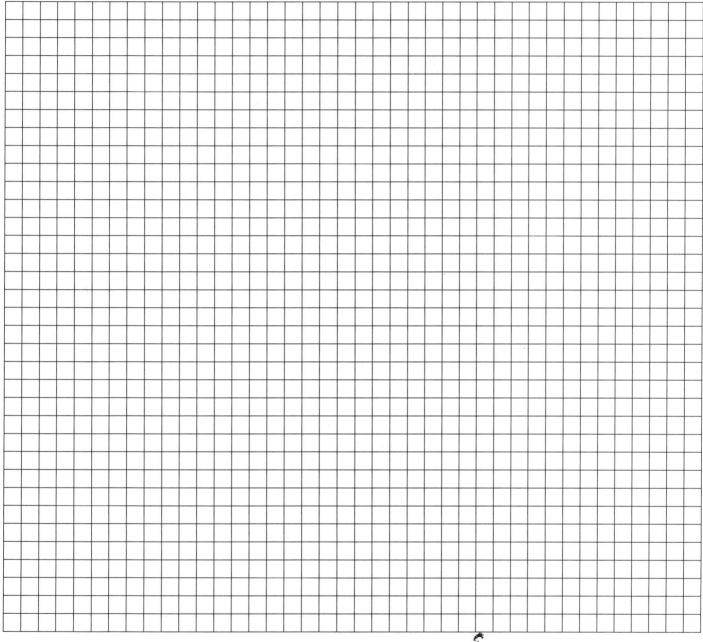

❏ bookcases

❏ tables

❏ teacher chair

❏ teacher desk

❏ student chairs

❏ student desks

❏ rugs

❏ computers

❏ electronic equipment

❏ electrical outlets

❏ windows

❏ door

❏ _____

❏ _____

❏ _____

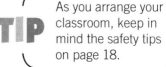

TIP As you arrange your classroom, keep in mind the safety tips on page 18.

Safety First

A good classroom plan incorporates safety precautions. Check to see that your room meets these safeguards.

❐ **All students' desks are visible.**

❐ **Window and door exits are clearly marked and unobstructed.**

❐ **High-traffic areas are free of congestion.**

❐ **Breakable items are stored or displayed in safe places.**

❐ **There are no frayed electrical cords or damaged plugs.**

❐ **Rugs have liners so they don't slide.**

❐ **Sharp or toxic items are stored in a safe place.**

❐ **Your name, class, and room number are clearly posted.**

❐ **Students have places to store their belongings.**

❐ **Floors are free of tripping hazards.**

❐ **Shelves are stable and not overloaded.**

 It's also a good idea to have a first aid kit on hand.

100 Essential Forms for New Teachers © 2011 by Linda Ward Beech, Scholastic Teaching Resources

Collect Stuff

Teachers tend to be experts at collecting things that might come in handy for projects. Use this chart as a starting place, then add your own ideas for collectibles.

Items	Possible Uses	My Ideas
paper bags	puppets, masks, wigs	
buttons	jewelry, eyes, collages	
hangers	mobiles, banners	
gift-wrap paper	paper chains, origami	
plastic meal trays	frames, printmaking, dioramas	
egg cartons	planters, animal sculptures	
plastic lids	coasters, frames	
ribbon	weaving, collages	

Section 2 Getting Acquainted

Overview: Here they come! A class of students will soon burst through the door, and you'll want to get to know them as quickly as possible. The pages in this section will help you get started.

Page 21: Class List
As your class list may change during the first weeks of school, you may want to keep it on the computer so you can add or delete names as necessary.

Page 22: Student Profile
Learning how students see themselves will help you understand them better too. Completing this profile also helps children focus on their role as students. Make copies of this page so that each student has one to fill out.

Page 23: Student Interview
As soon as possible (ideally, in the first few weeks of school), take each student aside for a brief interview. Talking to students in this way helps to show your interest in them and gives you a more complete picture of who they are.

Page 24: Profile From Home
Include a copy of this page in a packet of take-home materials to send home with each student at the end of the first day. Ask parents/guardians to complete the form and return it to you. This is a great way to involve families early in the year.

Page 25: Student Birthdays
Before making plans to celebrate students' birthdays, check to see if your school has special guidelines for observing these occasions.

Page 26: Partner Interview
Not only is it important to learn about each student, it's also beneficial that students learn about each other. Pair students and provide them with a copy of this page to conduct an interview. Later, have partners use the information to introduce each other to the class.

Pages 27–28: First-Day Activity 1; First-Day Activity 2
These activities are good icebreakers and will help students learn more about their classmates and classroom. Provide copies for students to use individually or in pairs.

Pages 29–30: Multiple Intelligences; Targeting Multiple Intelligences
The theory of multiple intelligences was developed by Dr. Howard Gardner and published in 1983. Teachers have found that tailoring instruction to students' different intelligences helps build self-esteem and confidence. The student profiles and interviews in this section may give you some early clues about students' different intelligences.

Class List

First Name	Last Name	Home Contact	Home Number

Student Profile

Name: _____

Check the things you enjoy at school.

____ reading books	____ working on the computer	____ math
____ science	____ music	____ writing stories
____ playing with friends	____ art	____ learning how to spell
____ social studies	____ helping out	____ physical education

other: _____

What do you like to do when you have free time in class?

_____

_____

Read each statement. Check the word that best tells about you.

I enjoy school.	___ yes	___ sometimes	___ no
I like to work in groups.	___ yes	___ sometimes	___ no
I work hard.	___ yes	___ sometimes	___ no
I like to help.	___ yes	___ sometimes	___ no
I like to learn.	___ yes	___ sometimes	___ no
I try to follow the rules.	___ yes	___ sometimes	___ no
I like to be a leader.	___ yes	___ sometimes	___ no

Student Interview

Make time to briefly interview each student early in the school year. Before each interview, explain that you would like to learn more about the student so you can get to know the class better.

Student name: _____

Tell me:
❑ what you like best and least about school
❑ about your favorite books
❑ about the people in your family
❑ what you usually do after school
❑ about something you are really proud of doing
❑ about something that is hard for you to do
❑ what you'd like to learn in school this year

Profile From Home

To parents and other caregivers: By completing this form, you will help me get to know your child better. Thank you!

How does your child feel about school in general?

_____

_____

What are your child's favorite subjects in school?

_____

_____

What are your child's least favorite subjects? Why?

_____

_____

What are your child's favorite pastimes and interests?

_____

_____

What are some things your child is especially proud of?

_____

_____

How often does your child read alone or with someone at home?

_____

_____

What else would you like me to know about your child?

_____

_____

Student name: _____

Parent/guardian name(s): _____

Daytime phone: _____ **Evening phone:** _____

100 Essential Forms for New Teachers © 2011 by Linda Ward Beech, Scholastic Teaching Resources

Student Birthdays

Use this handy chart to keep a record of each student's birthday. For most children, this is a very important day.

Partner Interview

Take turns with a partner to fill out this chart. Then talk about how you are alike and different.

Topic	Name of Partner 1 _____	Name of Partner 2 _____
Place you were born		
Brothers and sisters		
Favorite possession		
Favorite book		
Favorite sport		
Favorite animal		
Favorite food		
Favorite TV show		
Favorite color		

100 Essential Forms for New Teachers © 2011 by Linda Ward Beech, Scholastic Teaching Resources

First-Day Activity 1

Find a classmate who fits each description. Then, write the student's name on the line. You can use the same name only twice.

Name: _____

Find someone who:

1. has a birthday in March _____

2. is wearing something blue _____

3. went to camp this summer _____

4. has a cat _____

5. has a first name beginning with *S* _____

6. loves the color purple _____

7. likes chocolate ice cream best _____

8. can name the President of the U.S. _____

9. has more brothers than sisters _____

10. is wearing stripes _____

11. has a brother or sister in this school _____

12. wears glasses _____

13. has a red bookbag _____

14. can whistle a tune _____

First-Day Activity 2

Find something in the classroom that fits each description. Then write the items on the lines.

Name: _____

Find something:

1. that turns _____

2. made of metal _____

3. that makes noise _____

4. you can open _____

5. made of plastic _____

6. you can't reach _____

7. you can see through _____

8. made of wood _____

9. that snaps _____

10. that has corners _____

11. that has wheels _____

12. that is made of cardboard _____

13. that hangs _____

14. that holds books _____

Multiple Intelligences

Knowing how students learn enables you to draw on their strengths. The theory of multiple intelligences includes eight ways of learning. Although all students have a combination of intelligences, they usually excel in one or few areas.

Ways of Being Smart

Kind of Intelligence	Strengths	Students With These Strengths
Verbal-Linguistic Ease in producing language: reading, writing, telling stories, thinking in words	• reading • writing • talking • memorizing • working at puzzles	
Mathematical-Logical Can reason deductively or inductively: math, logic, problem solving, patterns	• working with numbers • solving problems • questioning • experimenting	
Spatial Can create visual-spatial representations and transfer them mentally or concretely	• reading maps and charts • drawing • doing puzzles and mazes • imagining	
Naturalist Able to recognize flora and fauna, make distinctions in the natural world	• exploring living things • working in nature	
Musical Shows sensitivity to pitch, timbre, rhythm of sounds	• singing • recalling melodies • playing musical instrument	
Bodily-Kinesthetic Uses body to solve problems, convey ideas and emotions	• athletics • dancing • acting • using tools	
Interpersonal Works effectively with others, understands their motivations	• leading • organizing • communicating • selling • resolving conflicts	
Intrapersonal Understands self, recognizes weaknesses and strengths	• working alone • reflecting • pursuing interests	

Targeting Multiple Intelligences

When planning a class unit or project, use a web like this to help you develop activities for each of the eight intelligences

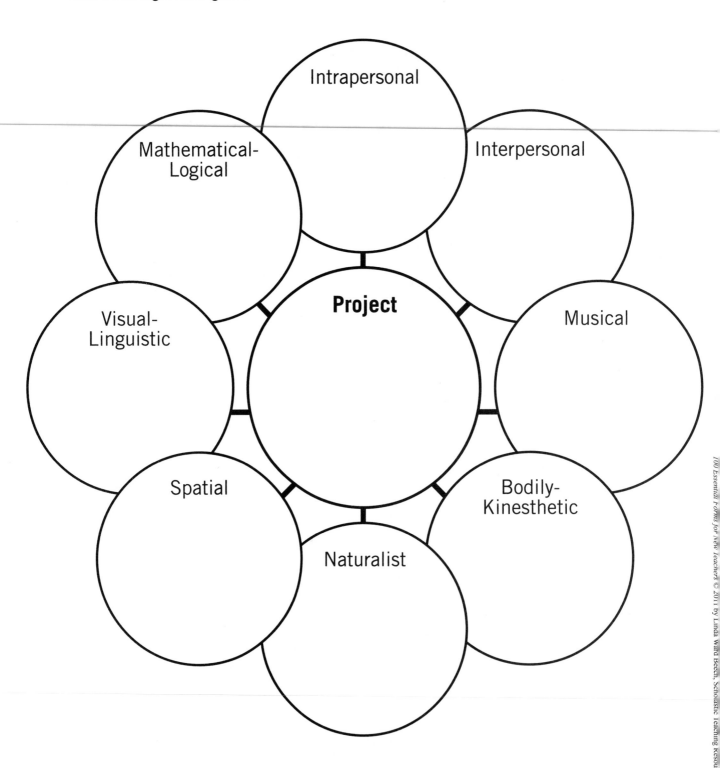

100 Essential Forms for New Teachers © 2011 by Linda Ward Beech, Scholastic Teaching Resources

Section 3 Plans & Procedures

Overview: Classroom management is an important partner to classroom teaching. The pages in this section will help you set up procedures and put plans in motion.

Page 32: Class Procedures
Create posters, signs, and other visual reminders of the classroom procedures you establish. Once students understand what is expected of them, you can spend more time teaching instead of managing.

Pages 33–34: Planning for the Week; Lesson Plan
Make multiple copies of these pages to use throughout the school year. You'll find it also comes in handy to complete these forms for substitutes.

Page 35: Classroom Chores Chart
Set up a system of chores that students can do to help out in the classroom. Then describe and model how each job should be done. Assign jobs to students on a rotating basis. Some teachers create a large chart on which to post the names of students assigned to chores each week.

Pages 36–37: Miscellaneous Tasks; Monthly Calendar
Use these forms to create systems for keeping track of "housekeeping" tasks and monthly events.

Page 38: Hall Passes
After you have made copies of the office and nurse station passes and cut them apart, invite students to color them. Keep a supply handy for instant use.

Page 39: Homework Helper
Distribute copies of this page to students to help them keep track of their homework assignments each week.

Class Procedures

A well–managed classroom has established procedures. Determine the procedures you will follow and teach them to students the first week of school. Use this checklist as a guideline.

Beginning Class

❑ Entering room   ❑ Lining up

❑ Putting away backpacks   ❑ Assigning student helpers

❑ Taking attendance   ❑ Using restroom

❑ Managing tardy students   ❑ Using drinking fountain or sink

❑ Reciting Pledge of Allegiance   ❑ Other: _____

❑ Using pencil sharpener

At Work

❑ Distributing materials   ❑ Monitoring group behavior

❑ Heading papers   ❑ Lining up for lunchtime/recess

❑ Signaling for student attention   ❑ Conducting fire drills

❑ Signaling for teacher attention   ❑ Managing free time

❑ Knowing what to do when classwork is done   ❑ Using the computer

❑ Completing and turning in homework   ❑ Throwing out trash

Ending Class

❑ Putting away materials   ❑ Leaving for the day/dismissal

❑ Cleaning up   ❑ Other: _____

Planning for the Week

Make multiple copies of this page so you can use it every week.

Week of _____

	LESSON NOTES	OBJECTIVES	MATERIALS
MONDAY Date:			
TUESDAY Date:			
WEDNESDAY Date:			
THURSDAY Date:			
FRIDAY Date:			

Lesson Plan

Using a planning sheet such as this will help you focus your lessons from start to finish.

Lesson Title	
Subject	
Objectives	
Materials	
Procedure	Intro 1. 2. 3. Conclusion
Homework	
Assessment	
Notes	

100 Essential Forms for New Teachers © 2011 by Linda Ward Beech, Scholastic Teaching Resources

Classroom Chores Chart

Most students enjoy helping out in the classroom. Use this page to record who is responsible for chores each week.

Job	Student	Week
Messenger		
Line Leader		
Paper/Materials Distributor		
Computer Monitor		
Trash/Recycling Monitor		
Flag Salute Leader		
Librarian		

Miscellaneous Tasks

A checklist like this is helpful in keeping track of who has completed various tasks such as turning in permission forms, notices, and money. List tasks on the slanted lines and check off the students who have completed them.

Month _____

Tasks

Students _____

Notes _____

100 Essential Forms for New Teachers © 2011 by Linda Ward Beech, Scholastic Teaching Resources

Monthly Calendar

Use copies of this calendar for keeping track of holidays, school events, school vacations, birthdays, and other important dates.

MONTH

	SUNDAY	SATURDAY	FRIDAY	THURSDAY	WEDNESDAY	TUESDAY	MONDAY

Hall Passes

Use copies of these passes when students need to visit the office or school nurse.

Office Pass

Date: _____

Student: _____

Teacher: _____

Room Number: _____

Nurse Station Pass

Date: _____

Student: _____

Teacher: _____

Room Number: _____

Homework Helper

Use this page to write down your homework each day. Put a check in the box when the work is done.

Name: _____

Monday

_____ ☐

_____ ☐

_____ ☐

_____ ☐

Tuesday

_____ ☐

_____ ☐

_____ ☐

_____ ☐

Wednesday

_____ ☐

_____ ☐

_____ ☐

_____ ☐

Thursday

_____ ☐

_____ ☐

_____ ☐

_____ ☐

Friday

_____ ☐

_____ ☐

_____ ☐

_____ ☐

Things to Bring to School

_____ ☐

_____ ☐

_____ ☐

_____ ☐

Section 4 Classroom Library

Overview: One of the most important areas in an elementary classroom is the library. Many teachers see it as the heart of effective literacy instruction. It is a place that fosters independent reading—a place where students learn and talk about the books they have chosen to read.

Page 41: Library Map
Set up a card system or other arrangement to keep track of the books that students borrow from the library.

Page 42: Reader Interest Inventory
Before introducing students to your classroom library, have them fill out this interest inventory. Use the completed forms to guide students to books they might enjoy.

Page 43: A "Just Right" Book Test
Many students need help in book selection for independent reading. Give them this page to help them choose appropriate books.

Page 44: Genre Chart
Provide copies of this page in your library to encourage students to try different kinds of books.

Page 45: Student Reading Record
Include copies of this Student Reading Record in your classroom library so students—and you—can keep track of the books they read.

Pages 46–47: Reading Contract for Fiction; Reading Contract for Nonfiction
Contracts provide a framework for independent reading. Duplicate the reading contracts on these pages and place them in your classroom library. Instruct students to complete a contract for each book they read.

Page 48: Checklist of Independent Reading Habits
Use this checklist to periodically record reading behavior exhibited in your classroom library.

Library Map

No matter how small the space, it's a good idea to organize your classroom library so students can find their way around. Display the map on this page or one that you create to remind students how your library is set up.

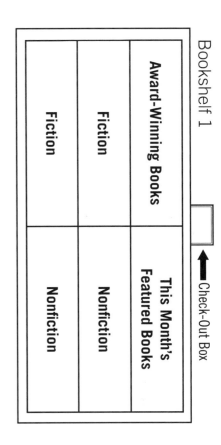

Bookshelf 1

Award-Winning Books	Fiction	Fiction
This Month's Featured Books	Nonfiction	Nonfiction

→ Check-Out Box

Bookshelf 2   ← Check-Out Box

Poetry	Theme
Leveled Readers	Leveled Readers
Reference	Series

TIP Instead of shelves, you can also use bins to store the books in your library.

41

Reader Interest Inventory

Circle the number that best tells how you feel about each statement.

Name: _____

	Often	Sometimes	Never
1. I like to read books with lots of pictures.	1	2	3
2. I like to read books about animals.	1	2	3
3. I like to read adventure stories.	1	2	3
4. I like to read make-believe stories.	1	2	3
5. I like to read sports stories.	1	2	3
6. I like to read funny stories.	1	2	3
7. I like to read books about kids my age.	1	2	3
8. I like to read books about nature.	1	2	3
9. I like to read books about famous people.	1	2	3
10. I like to read stories about long-ago times.	1	2	3
11. I like to read books in a series.	1	2	3
12. I like to read true stories.	1	2	3

A "Just Right" Book Test

Read each numbered question. Then answer the questions that follow. If your answers to these questions are mostly YES, your answer to the numbered question is also YES.

Name: _____

1. Is the book too easy?

Have you read the book before?	YES	NO
Can you read almost all of the words?	YES	NO
Does the book look easy to you?	YES	NO

2. Is the book just right?

Can you read the book without much help?	YES	NO
Can you read most of the words?	YES	NO
Is the story or subject of interest to you?	YES	NO

3. Is the book too hard?

Would you need lots of help to read the book?	YES	NO
Would you have trouble reading many words?	YES	NO
Do you think the story would confuse you?	YES	NO
Would you have to reread a lot of pages	YES	NO

Genre Chart

How many different kinds of books will you read? Write the name of the books you read under the correct heading.

Name: _____

KINDS OF BOOKS		
Picture Book	Make-Believe	Biography
Poetry	Funny	Reference
How-To	Long Ago	Mystery
Adventure	Fairy Tale, Myth, Folktale	Nonfiction

100 Essential Forms for New Teachers © 2011 by Linda Ward Beech, Scholastic Teaching Resources

Student Reading Record

Keep a record of the books you read. Write down the title, author, and date you finish each book.

Name: _____

BOOK TITLE	AUTHOR	DATE FINISHED

Reading Contract for Fiction

Sign your name on the line, then write the name of your book. Check off each box as you complete the activity.

Name: _____

Book title: _____

MY BOOK CONTRACT
❒ Read to yourself.
❒ Halfway through the book, make a prediction about the ending.
❒ Read a page to someone at home.
❒ Reread your favorite part.
❒ Write three questions to ask the author.   1.   2.   3.
❒ Make a poster to tell about the book.

100 Essential Forms for New Teachers © 2011 by Linda Ward Beech, Scholastic Teaching Resources

Reading Contract for Nonfiction

Sign your name on the line, then write the name of your book. Check off each box as you complete the activity.

Name: _____

Book title: _____

MY BOOK CONTRACT
❐ Read to yourself.
❐ Use the table of contents to find a topic.   Which topic did you choose? _____
❐ Read a passage to your teacher.
❐ Reread a part to understand it better.
❐ Write three questions based on facts in the book.   1.   2.   3.
❐ Make a web about a topic in the book.

Checklist of Independent Reading Habits

As students use the class library, record your observations of their independent reading habits. Make note of areas where help or improvement is needed.

Student name:_____ **Date:** _____

OBSERVATIONS	NOTES
Number of titles on Student Reading Record	
Variety of titles	
Variety of genres	
Selects books appropriate to reading level	
Gets started quickly	
Reads independently	
Self-helps before seeking assistance	
Shows pleasure in reading	
Completes reading contracts	
Shares responses to books with others	

Section 5 Curriculum Areas: Reading, Writing, Language Arts

Overview: The forms in this section will help you to both collect and provide information useful in teaching reading, writing, vocabulary, and spelling.

Page 50: Concepts of Print

Before students can begin to read, they need to master some basic concepts about print. Use this survey to determine if a child is unfamiliar with any of these concepts.

Pages 51–53: Early Reader Profile; Developing Reader Profile; Reader Attitude Survey

Use these pages to create profiles of students as readers. Write your comments on pages 51–52; students can complete page 53 on their own or with your help.

Pages 54–56: Fiction Reading Habits; Nonfiction Reading Habits; Think-Aloud Comprehension Strategies

It's important for students to learn to be active readers. Give students copies of these pages to use as helpful reminders when they read. Before giving out page 56, be sure to model how to think aloud while reading. Provide enough examples so students understand that they, too, can use these strategies to get more from their reading.

Pages 57–58: Retelling Fiction Checklist; Retelling Nonfiction Checklist

These forms are handy when you want to monitor reading comprehension on an informal basis. Make multiple copies and keep the completed forms in students' files.

Pages 59–60: Responding to Fiction; Responding to Nonfiction

Encourage students to use these forms to recall and think about what they have read. When you introduce these pages, use a completed form as a model for students.

Page 61: Writing Survey

Before giving writing assignments, have students complete this survey to give you an idea how they view this task. Plan to work with students in areas where they show weaknesses.

Pages 62–63: Word Study Checklist; Word Study Web

Provide copies of these pages to students to help them develop their vocabulary.

Pages 64–65: Spelling Survey; Spelling Checklist

Have students complete the survey before they attempt writing assignments. Model each strategy for attempting to spell words correctly. Suggest that students keep the checklist handy when working on writing assignments as it provides good strategies for spelling problems.

Concepts of Print

Use this informal procedure with prereaders to determine how well they handle books and attend to print

Student name:_____ **Date:** _____

Prompt	Response (✓ = correct)	Print Concept
Display the book and ask: "What's inside?"		book contains story, information; print contains message
Present book upside down, spine first and say: "Show me the front of this book. Then open it so we can read it together."		book layout
With book open to the first pages, say: "Point to where I should start reading."		directionality; where to begin
Then say: "Point to where my eye will go next on this page."		directionality; left-to-right progression
Say: "When I get to the end of this line, where will my eye go?"		directionality; return sweep
Turn the page and say: "Point to the top of the page. Point to the bottom. Point to the middle."		terminology: top, bottom, middle
Say: "Point to one letter."		terminology: letter
Say: "Point to one word."		terminology: word
Turn to a page with corresponding letters. Point to a capital letter and say: "Show me a small letter that is like this one."		matching uppercase and lowercase letters

Early Reader Profile

Use this form to identify the skills of your early readers.

Student name:_____ **Date:** _____

Early Reader	Comments
Knows print goes from left to right in English	
Reads pages in correct sequence	
Rereads miscues that disturb meaning	
Discusses and tells stories	
Demonstrates awareness of book language	
Recalls events of stories in logical sequence	
Makes eye/ear/voice matches	
Predicts outcomes of stories from pictures in book	
Makes predictions that are grammatically appropriate	
Rereads miscues that do not disturb meaning	
Distinguishes beginning, middle, final sounds in words	
Chooses books for free time	

Developing Reader Profile

Use this form to identify the skills of your developing readers.

Student name:_____ **Date:** _____

Developing Reader	Comments
Makes appropriate associations between letters and sounds	
Substitutes synonyms or close approximations for unfamiliar words	
Identifies rhyming words, common word structures, and families	
Uses knowledge of rhyming words, word structures, and word families to figure out unfamiliar words	
Rereads miscues that do not disturb meaning	
Understands dialogue markings	
Predicts from title, opening sentence, and/or first paragraph	
Recognizes and comments on story structure and text format	
Recalls literal information	
Makes inferences	
Relates own knowledge to story	
Comments on characters	
Reads for information	
Uses index, glossary, table of contents, etc.	

Reader Attitude Survey

Read each statement, then check the box that best describes your reading habits.

Name: _____

	Usually	Sometimes	Never
I feel good about how I read.	❏	❏	❏
I like to read by myself.	❏	❏	❏
I learn new things from reading.	❏	❏	❏
I like to read with other people.	❏	❏	❏
I think reading helps me with schoolwork.	❏	❏	❏
I think reading is fun.	❏	❏	❏
I like to choose books during free time.	❏	❏	❏
I like to use the library.	❏	❏	❏
I like to talk about books with friends.	❏	❏	❏
I like to read books at home.	❏	❏	❏
I like to receive books as gifts.	❏	❏	❏
I think reading is important.	❏	❏	❏

Fiction Reading Habits

Use this checklist of reading habits to help you get the most out of the fiction you read.

Name: _____

Before Reading . . .

❏ I look at the cover, title, and author of the book.

❏ I look at the pictures and/or chapter headings.

❏ I ask myself questions.

❏ I make predictions.

During Reading . . .

❏ I make pictures in my mind.

❏ I stop and check to see if I understand things.

❏ I reread parts I don't understand.

❏ I try to figure out words I don't know.

❏ I use the pictures to help me understand.

❏ I use what I already know to help me.

After Reading . . .

❏ I think about the ending.

❏ I think about my predictions.

❏ I speak, draw, or write my response.

❏ I reread favorite parts.

❏ I share my ideas about the book with others.

Nonfiction Reading Habits

Use this checklist of reading habits to help you get the most out of the nonfiction you read.

Name: _____

Before Reading . . .

❑ I think about why I am reading.

❑ I study the cover and title of the book.

❑ I think about the topic and what I already know about it.

❑ I ask myself questions.

❑ I make predictions about what I will learn.

During Reading . . .

❑ I stop and check to see if I understand things.

❑ I reread parts I don't understand.

❑ I try to figure out words I don't know.

❑ I use the pictures, headings, and captions to help me understand.

❑ I use what I already know to help me.

❑ I ask questions.

After Reading . . .

❑ I sum up what I read in my own words.

❑ I think about my predictions.

❑ I decide what the important ideas are.

❑ I reread to find details.

❑ I use the text to support my opinions.

Think-Aloud Comprehension Strategies

When you read, try using these Think-Alouds to help you understand the text.

Name: _____

PREDICT

I think

_____ will happen

because _____.

MAKE CONNECTIONS

This

_____ reminds me

of _____.

ASK QUESTIONS

What is happening?

What did I learn?

NEW WORDS

This is a new word for

me. It might mean

_____ because _____.

CHECK UNDERSTANDING

I am not sure of

_____. I will reread

this part.

Retelling Fiction Checklist

This checklist provides an informal way for you to monitor a student's comprehension.

Student name:_____ **Date:** _____

Book: _____

Task	Rating 4 = highest			
Identified and recalled setting	1	2	3	4
Identified and talked about main characters	1	2	3	4
Retold the sequence of story events correctly	1	2	3	4
Understood the story problem	1	2	3	4
Described the story climax and/or resolution	1	2	3	4
Expressed ideas clearly	1	2	3	4
Related characters and events to own experience	1	2	3	4
Drew conclusions about story	1	2	3	4
Needed little or no prompting	1	2	3	4

Retelling Nonfiction Checklist

This checklist provides an informal way for you to monitor a student's comprehension.

Student name: _____ **Date:** _____

Book: _____

Task	Rating 4 = highest
Identified the main idea(s)	1 2 3 4
Identified supporting details	1 2 3 4
Used or talked about information in text	1 2 3 4
Aware of features such as visuals, captions, maps	1 2 3 4
Expressed ideas clearly	1 2 3 4
Related information to prior knowledge	1 2 3 4
Summed up information	1 2 3 4
Drew conclusions from information	1 2 3 4
Needed little or no assistance	1 2 3 4

Responding to Fiction

Make a story map. Fill in this page to tell about a book you have read.

Name: _____

Story Map for _____
Setting
Characters
My favorite character is _____ because
Problem
Events
Outcome (how problem is solved and how story ends)
How I feel about the ending

Responding to Nonfiction

Fill in this page to tell about a nonfiction book you have read.

Name: _____

Book Title: _____
Topic
Author
Facts I learned: 1. 2. 3. 4.
I think these facts are important because
Important terms I learned are
Other things I would like to learn about this topic are

Writing Survey

Answer these questions to learn more about yourself as a writer.

Name: _____

When it comes to writing, what do you think your strengths are?

_____

_____

What do you think your weaknesses are?

_____

_____

Who are some of your favorite authors?

_____

_____

Read each statement. Check the word that best tells about you as a writer.

I think about what I will say first. _____ always _____ sometimes _____ never

I keep in mind who my readers will be. _____ always _____ sometimes _____ never

I express my ideas clearly. _____ always _____ sometimes _____ never

I write in complete sentences. _____ always _____ sometimes _____ never

I pay attention to spelling. _____ always _____ sometimes _____ never

I pay attention to capitalization and punctuation. _____ always _____ sometimes _____ never

I reread and revise my work to improve it. _____ always _____ sometimes _____ never

Word Study Checklist

Use this checklist when you find unfamiliar words in your reading.

Name: _____

When I come to a word I don't know . . .

❏ I look at the beginning letter or letters.

❏ I look at the last letters.

❏ I sound it out.

❏ I look for parts I know.

❏ I think about other words I know.

❏ I reread the sentence.

❏ I look for clues in the sentence or paragraph.

❏ I skip the word, read on, and come back to it later.

❏ I use the pictures to help me.

❏ I check:

Does it make sense?

Does it sound right?

Does it look right?

❏ I ask for help.

Word Study Web

When you come across a new word, use a web like this to help you learn the word.

Name: _____

I think it means . . .

My sentence with the word:

Dictionary meaning:

WORD

Antonym:

Sentence from book with the word:

Synonym:

Spelling Survey

Answer these questions to learn more about your spelling habits.

Name: _____

When it comes to spelling, what do you think your strengths are?

_____

_____

What do you think your weaknesses are?

_____

_____

What are some hard words you have learned to spell?

_____

_____

Spelling is important because

_____

_____

Read each statement. Check the word that best tells about you as a speller.

When I don't know how to spell a word, I

sound it out	____ always	____ sometimes	____ never
look in the dictionary	____ always	____ sometimes	____ never
try to recall spelling rules that I know	____ always	____ sometimes	____ never
use spell-check on the computer	____ always	____ sometimes	____ never
ask the teacher	____ always	____ sometimes	____ never

Spelling Checklist

Check the sentences that tell about your spelling habits.

Name: _____

☐ I try to spell unknown words.

☐ I write the sounds I hear in a word.

☐ I think about what the word looks like.

☐ I try to use spelling patterns that I know.

☐ I use spelling rules that I know.

☐ I use memory aids to help me spell some words.

☐ I decide if a word is in a word family that I know.

☐ I use the rules for plurals.

☐ I use the rules for endings such as *-ed* and *-ing*.

☐ I check my spelling when I write.

☐ I use a dictionary to help me.

☐ I try to use new spelling words in my writing.

Write some of your new spelling words here.

Section 6 Curriculum Areas: Math, Social Studies, Science

Overview: The forms in this section will help you to both collect and provide information useful in teaching math, social studies, and science.

Page 67: Math Interest Inventory
Ask students to complete this page to give you an idea how confident and careful they are when it comes to math.

Pages 68–72: Addition Chart; Multiplication Table; Geoboard; Grid (1 Inch); Grid (1 Centimeter)
Use copies of these page in math lessons throughout the year. On the addition chart, point out the addition sign in the top left corner. Show how to use the chart by choosing a number from the top row and one from the left-hand column. Trace down from the top number and right from the left number. The answer is the number where the row and column intersect. Follow the same procedure for the multiplication table. Use the geoboard for work with plane figures. Use the grids for graphs, charts, and finding the area or perimeter of figures.

Page 73: Tangrams
Make copies of this page and have students cut out the seven pieces. Use the tangrams for work with plane figures, congruency, and art projects.

Page 74: Bar Graph Template
Duplicate this template for students to use when they are making bar graphs.

Page 75: Social Studies Interest Inventory
Ask students to complete this page to give you an idea how aware they are of social studies topics.

Pages 76–77: United States Outline Map; World Outline Map
Make multiple copies of these maps to use in social studies lessons. On the CD, there is also a version of each map without the labels.

Page 78: Report Outline
Use this template to teach outlining. Complete an example to use as a model.

Page 79: Science Interest Inventory
Ask students to complete this page to give you an idea how knowledgeable and interested they are when it comes to science.

Math Interest Inventory

Answer these questions to learn more about you and math.

Name: _____

What do you think your strengths in math are?

_____

_____

What do you think your weaknesses are?

_____

_____

What are some ways that you use math in your everyday life?

_____

_____

Read each statement. Check the word that best tells about you and math.

I like to work and play with numbers.	____ always	____ sometimes	____ never
I read math symbols carefully.	____ always	____ sometimes	____ never
I read directions carefully.	____ always	____ sometimes	____ never
I read word problems carefully.	____ always	____ sometimes	____ never
I look for clue words to help me.	____ always	____ sometimes	____ never
I check my answers.	____ always	____ sometimes	____ never
I ask for help if I don't understand something.	____ always	____ sometimes	____ never

Addition Chart

Name: _____

+	0	1	2	3	4	5	6	7	8	9	10	11	12
0	0	1	2	3	4	5	6	7	8	9	10	11	12
1	1	2	3	4	5	6	7	8	9	10	11	12	13
2	2	3	4	5	6	7	8	9	10	11	12	13	14
3	3	4	5	6	7	8	9	10	11	12	13	14	15
4	4	5	6	7	8	9	10	11	12	13	14	15	16
5	5	6	7	8	9	10	11	12	13	14	15	16	17
6	6	7	8	9	10	11	12	13	14	15	16	17	18
7	7	8	9	10	11	12	13	14	15	16	17	18	19
8	8	9	10	11	12	13	14	15	16	17	18	19	20
9	9	10	11	12	13	14	15	16	17	18	19	20	21
10	10	11	12	13	14	15	16	17	18	19	20	21	22
11	11	12	13	14	15	16	17	18	19	20	21	22	23
12	12	13	14	15	16	17	18	19	20	21	22	23	24

Multiplication Table

Name: _____

X	0	1	2	3	4	5	6	7	8	9	10	11	12
0	0	0	0	0	0	0	0	0	0	0	0	0	0
1	0	1	2	3	4	5	6	7	8	9	10	11	12
2	0	2	4	6	8	10	12	14	16	18	20	22	24
3	0	3	6	9	12	15	18	21	24	27	30	33	36
4	0	4	8	12	16	20	24	28	32	36	40	44	48
5	0	5	10	15	20	25	30	35	40	45	50	55	60
6	0	6	12	18	24	30	36	42	48	54	60	66	72
7	0	7	14	21	28	35	42	49	56	63	70	77	84
8	0	8	16	24	32	40	48	56	64	72	80	88	96
9	0	9	18	27	36	45	54	63	72	81	90	99	108
10	0	10	20	30	40	50	60	70	80	90	100	110	120
11	0	11	22	33	44	55	66	77	88	99	110	121	132
12	0	12	24	36	48	60	72	84	96	108	120	132	144

Geoboard

Name: _____

100 Essential Forms for New Teachers © 2011 by Linda Ward Beech, Scholastic Teaching Resources

Grid (1 Inch)

Name: _____

Grid (1 Centimeter)

Name: _____

Tangrams

Name: _____

candle   cat   house

Bar Graph Template

Name: _____

Graph Title: _____

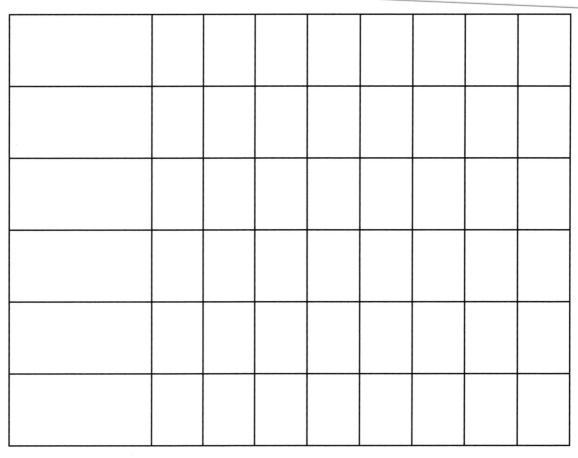

        1   2   3   4   5   6   7   8

100 Essential Forms for New Teachers © 2011 by Linda Ward Beech, Scholastic Teaching Resources

Social Studies Interest Inventory

Answer these questions to learn more about you and social studies.

Name: _____

Who is a famous historical figure that you admire? Why?

_____

_____

If you could live during a time in the past, when would it be? Why?

_____

_____

Where in the world would you like to visit? Why?

_____

_____

Read each statement. Circle the number that best tells about you and social studies. Number 1 is the least; number 4 is the most.

	Least			Most
I am interested in learning about other people.	1	2	3	4
I like learning about different cultures.	1	2	3	4
I like learning about different places.	1	2	3	4
I like learning about my community.	1	2	3	4
I like learning about past events.	1	2	3	4
I like working with others in a group.	1	2	3	4

United States Outline Map

CA

OR

WA

HI

NV

ID

AZ

UT

MT

AK

NM

CO

WY

TX

OK

KS

NE

SD

ND

MN

IA

WI

LA

AR

MO

IL

MI

MS

AL

TN

IN

KY

OH

WV

GA

SC

NC

VA

PA

NY

FL

VT

NH

MA

CT

RI

ME

NJ

DE

MD

DC

N

100 Essential Forms for New Teachers © 2011 by Linda Ward Beech, Scholastic Teaching Resources

World Outline Map

Arctic Ocean

Asia

Europe

Africa

Indian Ocean

Australia

Antarctica

Atlantic Ocean

North America

South America

Pacific Ocean

Report Outline

An outline is a good way to help you plan a report. Use this sheet to organize your ideas.

Name: _____

Topic: _____

I. Introduction: _____

    A. _____

    B. _____

II. _____

    A. _____

    B. _____

    C. _____

III. Summary and Conclusion: _____

    A. _____

    B. _____

    C. _____

Sources:

Science Interest Inventory

Answer these questions to learn more about you and science.

Name: _____

What are some ways that science affects your life?

_____

_____

What is an invention you would like to see in the future?

_____

_____

Name a famous scientist whom you admire.

_____

Circle the science topics that interest you.

animals	environment	weather	magnets
space	health	nature	plants
inventions	force and motion	computers	insects
oceans	heat and light	volcanoes	earthquakes

Read each statement. Circle the number that best tells about you and science. Number 1 is the least; number 4 is the most.

	Least			Most
I like to learn about new things in the world around me.	1	2	3	4
I like to do experiments.	1	2	3	4

Section 7 Assessment & Evaluation

Overview: To effectively assess and evaluate, you need a continuous stream of data. The forms in this section provide a framework for collecting and organizing some of this information.

Page 81: Student Grade Record
This multipurpose grade sheet can be adapted for different subjects.

Page 82: Self-Assessment
Students should have an opportunity to assess their own work and reflect on areas where improvement is needed. Use this form after you have returned tests and written assignments.

Page 83: Group Discussion Evaluation
Class or group discussions reflect student understanding, but not all students participate willingly. Use this checklist to identify students who need encouragement and guidance in oral discussions.

Pages 84–85: Progress Record; Conference Log
If you are working toward certain goals with a student, these forms will enable you to record progress and planned action.

Page 86: Observation Record
This overview of student behavior is invaluable at the beginning of the year and with new students who join the class during the year.

Page 87: Reading Skills Overview
You may wish to use this quick assessment checklist along with pages 51–53 in Section 5. It works well for reading lessons as well as for other curriculum areas such as social studies and science.

Page 88: Research Paper Evaluation
By using a list of assessment criteria or a scoring rubric, your grades on student papers will be more consistent. Always share these criteria beforehand so students know what is expected of them. Show students models of good and inadequate work so they understand how the criteria apply.

Pages 89–90: Project Assessment; Presentation Rubric
Provide students with a copy of the Project Assessment rubric so they can evaluate their work during and after projects. Use the Presentation Rubric when students give oral presentations.

Pages 91–92: Assessing Writing; Peer Comments
You may wish to create your own rubric based on items on this list that are appropriate for students' writing level. After students have shared their work, encourage listeners or readers to respond in writing with positive comments.

Pages 93–94: Achievement Award; Great Progress Award
Bestow these awards to deserving students to recognize achievement and improvement and to build self-esteem. Invite the recipients to color the awards with crayons or markers before taking them home.

Student Grade Record

Student name: _____ Subject: _____

Date	Assignment	Possible Points	Points Earned	Grade

Self-Assessment

Answer these questions to help you think about the work you are doing.

Name: _____ **Date:** _____

Subject: _____ **Assignment/Test:** _____

I earned this grade _____ **for the following reasons:**

_____

_____

I think the best thing about my work is _____

_____ .

Read each statement. Circle the word that best describes your work habits.

I listen carefully.	always	sometimes	never
I read directions carefully.	always	sometimes	never
I complete my classwork.	always	sometimes	never
I complete my homework.	always	sometimes	never
I do extra work.	always	sometimes	never
I ask for help if needed.	always	sometimes	never
I am willing to do things over.	always	sometimes	never

One way I think I can improve my work is _____

_____ .

Group Discussion Evaluation

By monitoring group discussions, you can identify those students who need guidance in how to participate.

Student name: _____ **Date:** _____

Topic: _____

KEY: R = rarely   S = sometimes   A = almost always   NO = not observed

_____ Contributes to discussion   _____ Dominates discussion

_____ Listens carefully and pays attention   _____ Uses prior knowledge or experience

_____ Values different ideas   _____ Addresses ideas presented by others

_____ Shows respect to others   _____ Asks meaningful questions

_____ Uses text for support   _____ Can help keep discussion flowing

_____ Rereads to point out details   _____ Draws reasonable conclusions

_____ Uses information from different sources   _____ Can summarize main point

_____ Shares ideas and cooperates   _____ Appears restless or disengaged

_____ Interrupts others   _____ Other: _____

Notes:

Progress Record

Monitoring progress in any subject or effort is important for both teachers and students.

Student name: _____ Subject: _____

Date	Working Toward	Planned Action	Comments

Conference Log

Use this page to keep notes from student conferences about projects they are working on or books they are reading.

Student name: _____

Date	Project or Book	Comments	Action

Observation Record

Try using this general assessment at the beginning of the year. The observations you make will help you plan instruction and measure progress during the rest of the year.

Name: _____ Date: _____

Observations	Comments
BEHAVIOR Does the student . . . • appear confident? Y N • make eye contact? Y N • show self-control? Y N • follow teacher requests? Y N	
WORK HABITS Does the student . . . • show initiative? Y N • stay on task? Y N • complete tasks on time? Y N • work neatly? Y N	
ORGANIZATION Does the student . . . • keep track of school materials? Y N • maintain desk neatly? Y N • follow directions well? Y N	
COMMUNICATION Does the student . . . • speak in complete sentences? Y N • speak clearly enough to be understood? Y N • hold informal conversations with others? Y N • demonstrate active listening? Y N	
COOPERATION Does the student . . . • work productively in a group? Y N • resolve social problems without adult intervention? Y N • interact well with peers? Y N • respond positively to peers? Y N	

Reading Skills Overview

Monitor reading behaviors by observing and recording how well students have mastered these skills.

Student name: _____ **Date:** _____

Does the student . . .

use picture clues in a text? ____ always ____ sometimes ____ never

refer back to text already read? ____ always ____ sometimes ____ never

read on? ____ always ____ sometimes ____ never

predict? ____ always ____ sometimes ____ never

recall sight words? ____ always ____ sometimes ____ never

sound out words? ____ always ____ sometimes ____ never

attend to print details? ____ always ____ sometimes ____ never

realize when something doesn't make sense? ____ always ____ sometimes ____ never

self-correct? ____ always ____ sometimes ____ never

make connections to text? ____ always ____ sometimes ____ never

Notes:

Research Paper Evaluation

Keeping notes about how well students meet the criteria for a research report allows you to identify strengths and weaknesses and to assess their mastery of the skills needed for the assignment.

Student name: _____ **Date:** _____

Topic of research paper: _____

Skills	Excellent	Very Good	Satisfactory	Unsatisfactory
Research Uses appropriate sources				
Uses adequate number of sources				
Lists sources in bibliography				
Writing Includes strong introduction				
Relates all paragraphs to topic				
Shows good understanding of topic				
Uses paraphrases and quotations				
Mechanics Proofreads for spelling, capitalization, punctuation				
Avoids grammatical and usage errors				

Project Assessment

As you work on your project, rate your progress. Use your ratings to help you improve the final outcome. Then when you're finished, answer the questions at the bottom of the page.

Name: _____ **Date:** _____

Topic: _____

KEY: 4 = excellent   3 = good   2 = fair   1 = poor

DURING PROJECT WORK

Points to Rate	My Rating
Choice of topic	_____
Doing research	_____
Taking notes	_____
Planning and organizing	_____
Imagination and creativity	_____
Finding materials for visual aids	_____
Neatness of work	_____
Meeting deadlines for each step	_____

WHEN PROJECT IS COMPLETED

What do you think is the best thing about your project?

_____

_____

How might you improve your work on the next project?

_____

_____

Presentation Rubric

Use this rubric to assess student presentations, including creative writing, research reports, projects, and other assignments.

Student name: _____ **Date:** _____

Presentation: _____

CRITERIA	Excellent	Very Good	Fair	Poor
Presenter is well prepared.				
Information is easily understood.				
Voice volume is appropriate.				
Makes eye contact with audience.				
Enunciates well and speaks clearly.				
Speaks with expression.				
Speaks with confidence.				
Avoids fidgeting, swaying, or other distracting movements.				
Paces speech well.				

Comments: _____

_____

_____

Assessing Writing

When students turn in writing assignments, use this checklist to help you assess their work.

Student name: _____ **Date:** _____

❏ Shows positive attitude toward writing.

❏ Uses a wide range of words.

❏ Uses appropriate words.

❏ Writes complete sentences.

❏ Uses topic or main idea sentences in nonfiction writing.

❏ Includes details, examples, and quotations to support ideas.

❏ Develops characters, setting, and plot in fiction pieces.

❏ Shows conflict in fiction pieces.

❏ Uses imagery.

❏ Attends to mechanics, including capitalization and punctuation.

❏ Attends to usage.

❏ Revises texts.

❏ Edits own work.

❏ Participates in peer conferences.

❏ Incorporates suggestions of others.

❏ Writes in more than one genre.

❏ Uses computer.

Peer Comments

Writers need feedback from readers. Please tell the author something you liked about this story.

Title: _____

Author: _____

Readers	Comments

Achievement Award

Achievement Award

presented to

Student

in recognition for

Teacher

Date

Great Progress Award

✂ ....

Great Progress Award

presented to

_____
Student

for improvement in

_____

_____
Teacher

_____
Date

Section 8 Preparing for Substitutes

Overview: It's not easy to walk into a classroom as a substitute teacher, so you'll want to offer your colleagues as much help as you can. Keep in mind, too, that the way your students react to a substitute is a reflection on you. If you know in advance that you'll be absent, be sure to alert them and communicate your expectations.

Page 96: Substitute Information Sheet
You can make the substitute's job easier and more effective if you prepare in advance for the possibility of your absence. Begin by using this form to record where things are kept. Set up a substitute file in which to keep this page and other information.

Page 97: Substitute Checklist
Use this checklist to help you organize materials and information to have on hand for substitutes.

Page 98: Schedule for Substitutes
Leave a copy of the schedule the substitute will follow in your absence.

Page 99: Feedback From Substitutes
Ask substitutes to complete this form to give you an idea of how things went in your absence.

Substitute Information Sheet

Teacher's name: _____ Class: _____ Room: _____

Contact information: _____

School: _____ Principal: _____

Where to Find . . .

Teacher's binder: _____

Class list: _____

Lesson plans: _____

Teacher's editions: _____

Curriculum guides: _____

Class list: _____

Seating plan: _____

Attendance folder: _____

School timetable: _____

Paper and other supplies: _____

Photocopy machine: _____ Access number: _____

Audiovisual equipment: _____

Emergency procedure information: _____

Staff restroom: _____

Teachers' lounge: _____

Teacher mailbox: _____

Substitute Checklist

The more information you give a substitute about your classroom management procedures, the more successful he or she will be in your absence. Use this list to help you anticipate a substitute's needs.

☐ Leave a class seating chart including any arrangements you have for small-group activities.

☐ Identify any special-needs students and describe the classroom management techniques that work best for them.

☐ Describe daily procedures such as the opening of the school day, using restroom passes, using the pencil sharpener, cleaning up, and class dismissal.

☐ Make a list of favorite books that the substitute might read aloud.

☐ Direct the substitute to reproducibles or other activities that might be used to fill brief periods, such as before the bell rings or when students finish an assignment early.

☐ Leave a form (see page 99) for the substitute to fill out outlining how the day went.

☐ Include a daily schedule (see page 98); be sure to indicate when students who work with specialists will be pulled from class.

☐ Prepare detailed lesson plans for the substitute to use.

☐ Make a list of students who would be particularly helpful.

☐ If possible, prepare your class ahead of time for your absence.

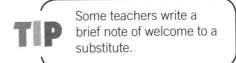

TIP Some teachers write a brief note of welcome to a substitute.

Schedule for Substitutes

Teacher's name: _____

Teaching Schedule

Period	Time	Subject	Room
1			
2			
3			
4			
5			
6			
7			

Notes

_____

_____

_____

Helpful Teachers You Might Consult

Teacher   **Room**

_____   _____

_____   _____

_____   _____

Feedback From Substitutes

To My Substitute:
Many thanks for teaching my class while I was away. It would be very helpful if you would complete this page summarizing your experience.

Teacher: _____

Assigned work was: ☐ completed   ☐ not completed

_____

_____

Class behavior was:

☐ excellent   ☐ courteous   ☐ cooperative   ☐ discourteous   ☐ uncooperative

_____

_____

It would be helpful next time if _____

_____

_____

Absent Students	Helpful Students	Disruptive Students
_____	_____	_____
_____	_____	_____
_____	_____	_____
_____	_____	_____

Substitute teacher: _____   **Date:** _____

Section 9 Home-School Connection

Overview: Parents are important partners when it comes to educating children. The forms in this section will help you get off to a good start with students' caretakers and will also aid you in keeping the lines of communication open throughout the year.

Page 101: Introductory Letter Home
Let parents know that they can help. Include this or a similar letter in a packet of materials that students take home during the first days of school. (See page 24 for another send-home page.)

Pages 102–105: Parent Meeting Checklist; Conference Questionnaire; Parent Conference Notes; Teacher Conference Notes
Preparation is key before a parent-teacher conference. Use the Parent Meeting Checklist to help you organize each individual conference. If you choose to use the Conference Questionnaire, send it home before the conference so parents have a chance to complete it. The questionnaire also serves as a reminder of the upcoming conference. Alternatively, you may decide to use the Parent Conference Notes and the Teacher Conference Notes. Both the parent and the teacher complete part of these before the meeting and add comments during it.

Page 106: Reading Letter
At some point during the first months of school, take the opportunity to send this letter about independent reading to parents.

Page 107: Parent Newsletter
A newsletter is a great way to keep family members informed. You might add photos or student artwork.

Pages 108–109: Areas of Concern; Good News and Bad News
It's important to keep the lines of communication with parents open at all times. The notes on these Pages will help you keep families informed. For additional positive demonstrations of support, you can also send home the student awards on pages 93 and 94.

Page 110: Open House Checklist
Open House is coming soon. Are you ready? Preparation and organization can make this event a positive and successful evening. Start with this checklist.

Page 111: Field Trip Permission Form
Before taking students on field trips, check with the office regarding school policies. When sending home the permission form, be sure to fill in the destination and date on the bottom portion.

Pages 112–113: Parent Involvement; Parents as Volunteers
Parents can be highly effective partners when it comes to student learning. Use these pages as guidelines to welcome and encourage parental involvement.

Introductory Letter Home

Reach out to parents during the first few days of school. Enlist their cooperation and support by sending home a letter like this.

Dear Parents and Guardians:

I look forward to teaching your child this coming year and want our time together to be as productive as possible. I would like to enlist your help. Below are a few suggestions that can help your child have success as a learner.

- Make sure your child has a good attendance record. Missing school often means that children fall behind.

- Set up a quiet place where your child can read and do homework. Establish a regular time for these activities.

- Encourage your child to discuss homework assignments.

- Ask to see graded papers and completed assignments that your child brings home.

- Be sure your child gets eight to nine hours of sleep at night.

- Keep your child healthy by providing a balanced diet and making sure that exercise is a regular part of his or her day.

- Please notify me of any medical or other problems.

- Most of all, encourage your child and express your pride in his or her efforts and accomplishments.

Many thanks for your support. I am confident that our efforts will make a difference.

Sincerely,

_____

Parent Meeting Checklist

You have scheduled individual parent conferences. Now you want to be sure they will go smoothly. Use this checklist to help you prepare.

- ☐ Identify what you hope to accomplish. Include any problems that need to be addressed.

- ☐ Plan to open the meeting with a positive statement about the student.

- ☐ Beforehand, clarify who is attending the conference, their relationship to the student, and their exact name(s). Don't assume that surnames will always be the same as the student's.

- ☐ Collect pertinent data to share, including a grade sheet for the student, a sample of the student's work, and a record of behaviors or concerns.

- ☐ Be prepared to offer two or three specific suggestions for parents to implement at home to help the student.

- ☐ Encourage parents to return their completed Conference Questionnaire (see page 103) a day or two prior to the conference. Prepare responses for any concerns or questions that they have raised.

- ☐ Have a calender available if a follow-up conference needs to be scheduled.

- ☐ Bring your completed Conference Notes form to the meeting and remind parents to bring theirs (see pages 104–105).

 TIP   Maintain a professional demeanor during parent conferences and avoid using educational jargon.

Conference Questionnaire

You may wish to have parents answer this questionnaire before a school conference.

To the parents/guardians of _____

From: _____

Your parent-teacher conference is scheduled for _____ at _____ in room _____ at the school. Please answer the questions that you would like to address at the meeting and return this sheet _____ days prior to the conference. Thank you!

Student name: _____

What academic goals would you like your child to achieve this year?

_____

_____

Do you have any specific areas of concern regarding your child's work?

_____

_____

Are there any health issues you would like me to be aware of?

_____

_____

Are there any familial/personal issues that may affect your child that you would like me to be aware of?

_____

_____

Does your child have concerns that you would like to discuss?

_____

_____

Are there any other issues you wish to explore?

_____

_____

Parent Conference Notes

Student name: _____

Parent(s): _____

Conference date: _____ **Class/Grade:** _____

Strengths and Needs Observed at Home	Comments at Conference
Academic Strengths	
Academic Needs	
Social Strengths	
Social Needs	

Teacher Conference Notes

Student name: _____

Teacher: _____

Conference Date: _____ **Class/Grade:** _____

Strengths and Needs Observed at School	Comments at Conference
Academic Strengths	
Academic Needs	
Social Strengths	
Social Needs	

Reading Letter

To promote reading, you'll want the support of parents and others at home. Duplicate the letter below to enlist their involvement.

Date: _____

Dear: _____,

As your child acquires new reading skills in class, we also want to promote independent reading. Research has shown that independent reading helps students maintain their momentum; it helps to create fluent and confident readers. It also helps students do better in other subject areas. In other words, as with many other skills, practice improves performance.

We have a library of books for independent reading in our school. I will be encouraging your child to select books for this purpose on an ongoing basis. You can help, too.

• Encourage your child to read to you or with you at night.

• Ask about the books your child is reading on a regular basis.

• Be a reading role model. Let your child see you and other family members reading books, newspapers, magazines, and material from the Internet. Help your child understand that independent reading is an important part of your life.

• Help your child build a personal library at home.

• Make frequent trips to the library or used-books sales with your child.

My thanks for your support in this endeavor. I sincerely believe that helping your child become a lifelong reader will make his or her life richer and more rewarding.

Yours truly,

_____

Parent Newsletter

Add information to this time-saving form to create a brief newsletter to send home on a monthly basis.

NEWS FROM CLASS _____

Date: _____ Teacher: _____

This month we studied:

Ask your child to tell you about . . .

Upcoming tests and/or projects will be . . .

Other things we are doing include:

Areas of Concern

At times you will need to bring parents up to date on areas of concern regarding a student. Consider using a form such as this.

✂ ....

Student: _____ **Date:** _____

Dear _____ ,

I want to alert you to the following area of concern regarding:

❏ Tardiness: Your child has been late _____ days this (month, quarter, semester).

❏ Absences: Your child has had _____ absences this (month, quarter, semester).

❏ Academics: Your child has missed _____ assignments this (month, quarter, semester).

❏ Behavior: Your child has been disruptive in class _____ times this (month, quarter, semester).

❏ Other: _____

Teacher Comments:

_____

_____

Please sign this report and return it to me. If you would like to contact me to discuss your child's

progress, you can reach me at _____

or (e-mail) _____. I hope that by working together, we can help

your child resolve this issue.

Parent/Guardian Signature: _____

Parent Comments:

_____

_____

_____

Good News and Bad News

These forms make it easy to keep parents informed.

Good News!

To: _____

(parent/guardian's name)

Re: _____

(student's name)

From: _____

(teacher's name)

I am so pleased to tell you that _____

_____

_____

_____   _____
(signature)   (date)

Homework Alert!

To: _____

(parent/guardian's name)

Re: _____

(student's name)

From: _____

(teacher's name)

Just a quick note to keep you informed that _____

❏ did not turn in homework   ❏ homework was incomplete   ❏ homework was late

Please sign and return this notice. You may reach me at _____
if you have any questions.

Parent Comments: _____

_____

Parent Signature: _____

Open House Checklist

Open House usually occurs early in the school year. It's important to make a good first impression. Use the tips on this checklist to help you prepare.

- ❐ Plan to dress in a professional manner.

- ❐ Prepare opening remarks that include a warm welcome, a thank-you to parents for coming, and some positive remarks about the year ahead.

- ❐ Be ready to introduce yourself and briefly explain your general philosophy of teaching and learning and your expectations of students.

- ❐ Have available examples of the texts and basic materials that students will use. Plan to discuss each briefly.

- ❐ Choose a few important class procedures and activities to describe.

- ❐ Create bulletin boards and other areas to show off student work. Make sure all students are represented.

- ❐ Develop a few suggestions (see pages 101 and 106) for ways that parents can help at home.

- ❐ Allow time in your presentation for questions.

- ❐ Create a sign-up sheet for individual parent conferences at a later date.

 TIP Where appropriate, inject humor into your presentation. Remember, parents are as nervous as you are!

Field Trip Permission Form

Dear Parent/Guardian:

Our class is going on a field trip to _____.

Date: _____

Departure time: _____ Return time: _____

Method of transportation: _____

The trip will allow students to: _____

_____.

Cost to student: _____

Items required: _____

Suggested attire: _____

Other information: _____

Supervising staff: _____

PLEASE RETURN THIS PORTION TO YOUR CHILD'S TEACHER BY _____

I give permission for _____ to participate

(student name)

in the field trip to _____ on _____.

Parent/Guardian Name: _____

(please print)

Parent/Guardian Signature: _____

Telephone: _____ e-mail: _____

Parent Involvement

How involved are parents in your school? Use this checklist to get an idea of areas where involvement could be improved.

	YES	NO
The school has a parent room or place where parents can gather.	☐	☐
Efforts are made to involve culturally diverse parents.	☐	☐
Communication between teachers and parents is frequent and effective.	☐	☐
The school has clearly defined policies regarding parental involvement.	☐	☐
Training programs for parents are available.	☐	☐
The businesses in the community are involved in the school.	☐	☐
Parents are asked about their child's thinking and behavior.	☐	☐
Parents routinely work in classrooms with students on learning activities.	☐	☐
Parents are promptly notified about problems involving their children.	☐	☐
School staff members are aware of cultural and language barriers.	☐	☐

Notes:

Parents as Volunteers

Parent volunteers can make a big difference in the classroom. Use this form to invite parents to lend their help.

Name: _____

Phone: _____ e-mail: _____

Student name: _____

Work preferences: Check all that apply.

____ Story-time reading   ____ Art projects

____ Snacks   ____ Field trips

____ Working one on one   ____ Music

____ Video recording   ____ Constructing bulletin boards

____ Small-group work   ____ Computer

____ Other: _____
                            (please specify)

_____

Day or days available: _____

Times available: _____

Section 10 For You, the Teacher

Overview: By nature of their work, teachers are givers, but they too need praise and support. Use these pages to reflect on your work, take pride in your strengths, manage stress, and develop in your profession.

Page 115: Strength Assessment
The traits listed on this page are helpful in the classroom as well as in many other kinds of work. Use the back of the page to list other strengths you have. After completing the page, spend time thinking about more ways in which you can use your strengths in the classroom. Consider also how you can develop some of the traits you did not check.

Page 116: Managing Stress
Teaching can be a demanding occupation. It's easy to let stress take over. As a reminder that you need to handle stress, place a copy of this page on your refrigerator or other prominent place.

Page 117: Résumé Notes
It's always a good idea to keep your professional résumé up to date. Use this sheet to make notes before organizing your résumé and making changes.

Page 118: Personal Reflections
It's helpful to step back from your work and reflect once in a while. If you do this several times a year, you should be able to see progress and growth.

Strength Assessment

Put a check next to each of the traits below that are true of you. Give an example of how this trait is evident in some aspect of your work.

❐ Effective leader

_____

_____

❐ Problem solver

_____

_____

❐ Able to change

_____

_____

❐ Self-starter

_____

_____

❐ Self-disciplined

_____

_____

❐ Team player

_____

_____

❐ Hard worker

_____

_____

❐ Honest and sincere

_____

_____

❐ Able to think outside the box

_____

_____

❐ Dependable

_____

_____

Managing Stress

Keep these tips where you can see them every day. Add your own stress strategies and ask fellow workers to share theirs.

STRESS STRATEGIES

☐ Recognize that stress is a daily part of life for everyone. You can handle it.

☐ Give yourself credit; keep small successes in mind and avoid focusing only on the negative things.

☐ Set realistic goals.

☐ Schedule fun into your day—something to look forward to.

☐ Laugh!

☐ Share ups and downs with colleagues who understand.

☐ After school, unwind with a walk, a few minutes alone, or a cup of coffee with a friend before facing responsibilities at home.

☐ Build time during the school year for your hobbies and other interests.

☐ Learn and use relaxation methods.

☐ Exercise regularly.

☐ Eat well.

☐ Get enough sleep.

☐ Regretfully decline too many commitments and duties.

☐ Keep laughing.

Résumé Notes

Use this page to jot down notes for your professional résumé.

Name/Address	Goals
Career Objective	Areas of Specialty/Skills
Education	Experience
Employment	Affiliations
Committees	Awards/Honors
Personal Information	References

Personal Reflections

From time to time, take a moment to reflect on your work as a teacher.

Date: _____

What am I doing that is successful? Why is this working?

_____

_____

What problems or issues do I still need to work out? How will I do that?

_____

_____

What is the hardest part of this job for me?

_____

_____

What is the most satisfying part?

_____

_____

What can I do to improve my performance?

_____

_____

How would I rate my working conditions? What can I do to change them?

_____

_____

Section 11 Graphic Organizers

Overview: Graphic organizers have multiple uses. They are especially helpful in sorting and identifying information. Many students are visual learners and greatly benefit from using graphic organizers to process information. You'll find common organizers on the following pages. You can duplicate these and use them over and over again. You can also enlarge them.

Page 120: Venn Diagram

A Venn diagram is useful in making comparisons. Students write the two things being compared on the lines in the two ovals. Information that's true of both items goes in the overlapping section of the ovals. Points of comparison that differ go under the appropriate headings in each oval.

Page 121: K-W-L Chart

The initials for this chart stand for **K**now, **W**ant to Know, and **L**earned. These charts are helpful at the beginning of a new unit of study to activate prior knowledge and to stimulate further investigation. Students list what they know under **K,** what they want to know under **W,** and when the unit of study is over, what they learned under **L.**

Page 122: Idea Web

An idea or concept web focuses on main ideas and supporting details. It can also be used as a word web for vocabulary lessons. The topic or word is always listed in the center of the web.

Page 123–124: Sequential Chart; Timeline

These charts are useful to show events that follow a sequence, such as steps in a process. A timeline presents a series of events in chronological order.

Page 125: Problem/Solution Chart

This chart helps students understand how problems and solutions are resolved.

Page 126: Cause-and-Effect Chart

This type of chart helps students identify relationships between events, useful in reading, social studies, and science lessons. The chart on this page shows one cause with several effects; you might also make a chart that shows several causes with one or more effects.

Page 127: Hierarchical Chart

A hierarchical chart is helpful in organizing and classifying information. Students write the main topic in the top space and the subtopics below it. Details for each subtopic go in the smallest spaces.

Page 128: Matrix

A matrix is useful for comparing and contrasting objects in science. Students write the criteria in the spaces at the top and the things they are comparing along the left side.

Venn Diagram

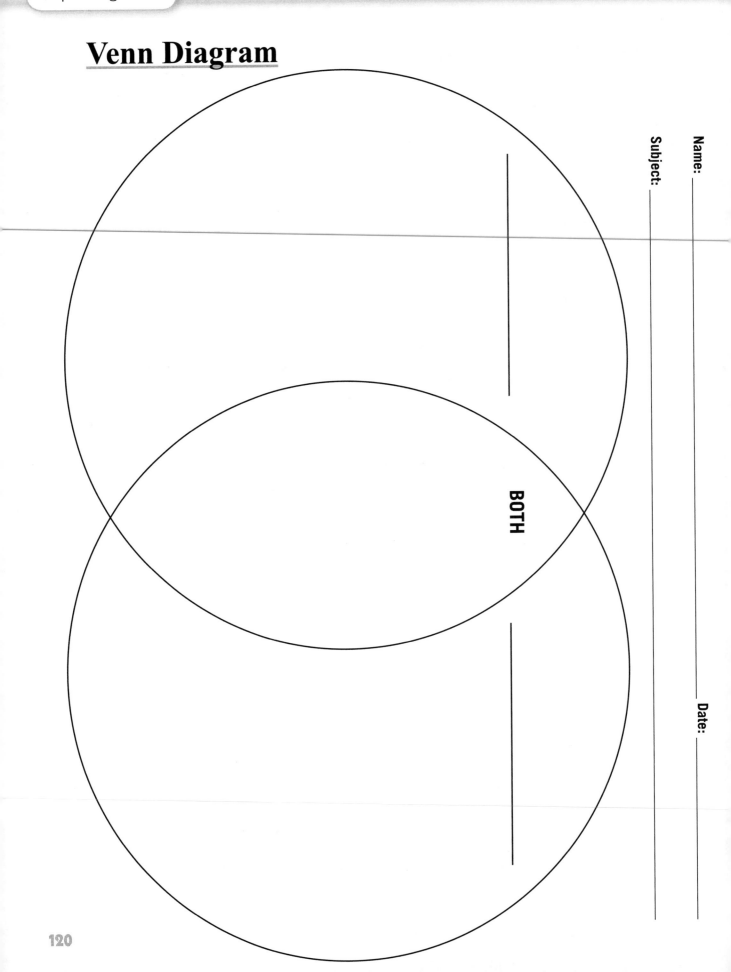

Name: _____ Date: _____

Subject: _____

BOTH

K-W-L Chart

Name: _____ **Date:** _____

Subject: _____

K = Know	W = Want to Know	L = Learned

Idea Web

Name: _____ **Date:** _____

Subject: _____

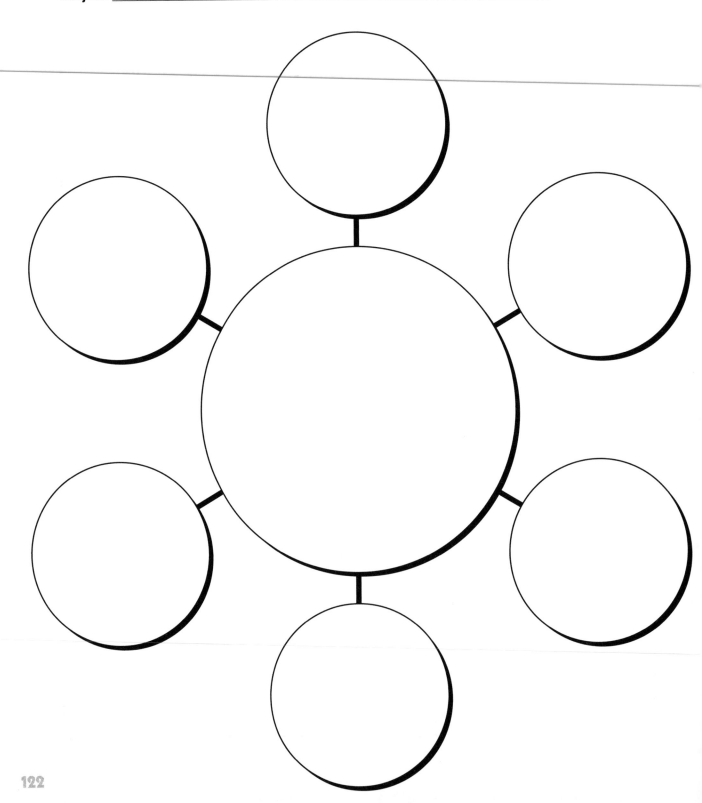

Sequential Chart

Name: _____

Subject: _____

Date: _____

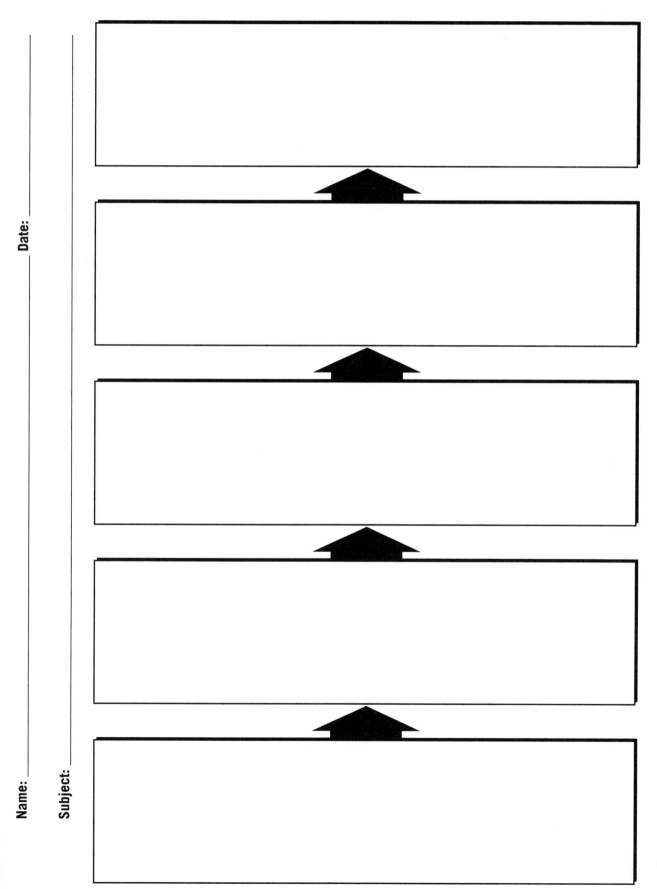

Timeline

Name: _____ Date: _____

Subject: _____

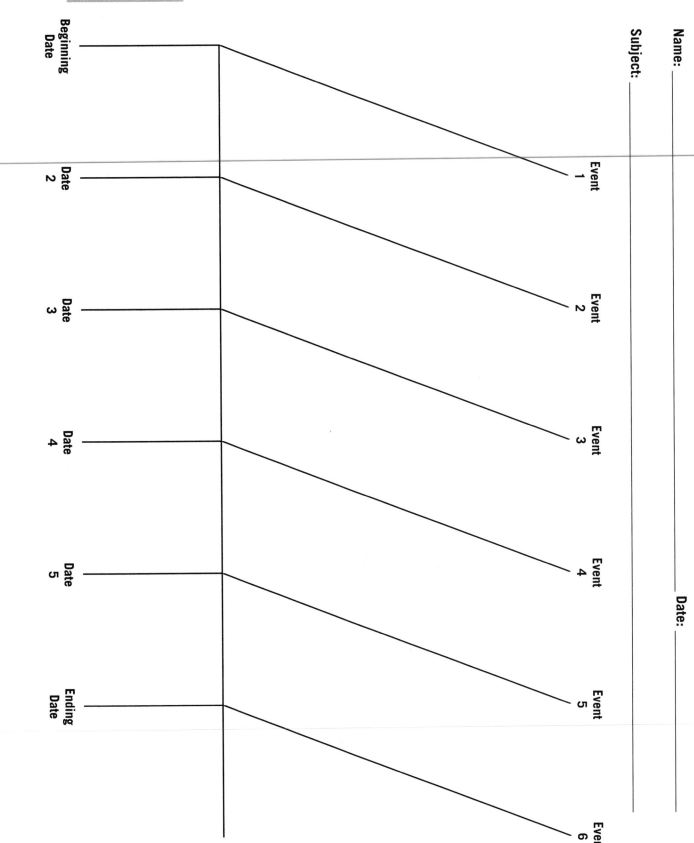

Beginning Date

Date 2

Date 3

Date 4

Date 5

Ending Date

Event 1

Event 2

Event 3

Event 4

Event 5

Event 6

Problem/Solution Chart

Name: _____ Date: _____

Problem

Attempted Solution

End Result

Cause-and-Effect Chart

Name: _____ Date: _____

Subject: _____

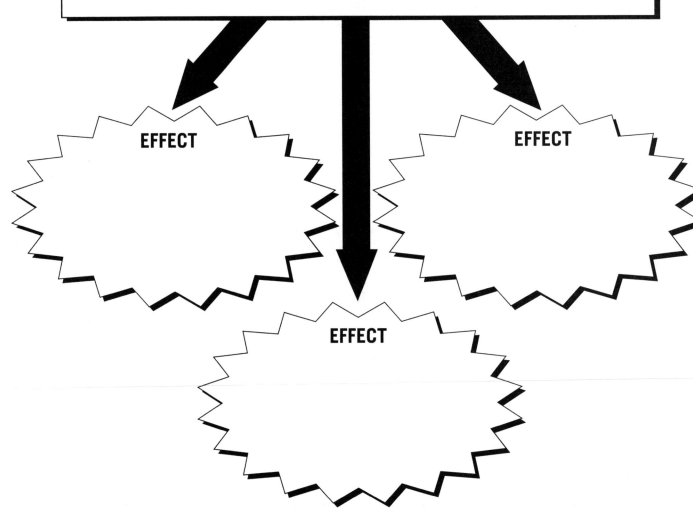

CAUSE

EFFECT

EFFECT

EFFECT

Hierarchical Chart

Name: _____ **Date:** _____

Subject: _____

Matrix

Name: _____ **Date:** _____

Subject: _____
